Guide to a Healthy Romance

Unlock the Mystery of Love

Donna E. Knight

ISBN: 978-1-4834-8294-1 (sc)
ISBN: 978-1-4834-8293-4 (e)

Library of Congress Control Number: 2018903398

Lulu Publishing Services rev. date: 3/13/2018

CONTENTS

INTRODUCTION

Love Happens all the time. Love isn't complex, it is simple but the process to achieve and maintain love in a committed relationship is the more complicated aspect. Love happens spontaneously because we are our own version of Love. Love is manifesting right now while you are reading this book.

Love is a thing (noun) not an action (verb). When we say we "love" someone; we are using love as a verb but what we are really saying is "You have a special place in my heart and I care about you deeply." Love is an emotional state. The action is a manifestation of the *thing*. For example, when my husband bought me a perfume I really liked, it was a simple act; but the fact that he bought it because of how much I liked it and talked about it and that he was paying attention to how much it meant to me, made the perfume priceless. The love he feels for me was shown through the act of buying the perfume.

Some men and women may believe their mate is going to come prepackaged in perfection of love – this is far from the truth. If this were the case we wouldn't need this book, dating websites, marriage counselors, or all the other mechanisms we use to find love or something like it. It takes a conscious effort to build a solid foundation in any relationship and maintain the true essence of love. We can feel love, but it is not easy to see. Love is invisible. Love is displayed through actions and those actions make love visible. Love is made visible through people. For this reason, again, we are love.

It may feel like true love is unobtainable because we fail in our attempts to obtain it. We all want, need, and desire love. We were created with this innate need to give and receive love, but the fact that it seems hard to find leads us to believe we can somehow exist without it. Truthfully, love isn't hard to find, it's hard to see.

Love is at the core of our existence and is present even when we are not aware. We are love. However, our life experience shapes how we express love or how we make it visible. This is the reason we have different expectations of how love or a relationship should go because we all express love differently. Some people are more affectionate than others; for example, some people are huggers, they love to give hugs. Some people are passionate. Some people are very romantic. But if a person doesn't show as much compassion or romance as another person, it doesn't mean they feel the emotion any less. They just express the feeling differently. The different expressions of love lead to the complexities of relationships.

The word *relationship* is used vaguely. What does it mean when someone says he or she is "in a relationship"? Does that mean "I'm taken"? Does it mean "I like the person I'm with, but other people still stand a chance"? The truth is, it means whatever you make it mean. People interpret romantic relationships in various ways and with various terms—friends with benefits, bed buddies, cuddle buddies, secret lover, significant other, etc. This often is done to relieve some of the stress that comes with exactly defining the relationship. Your relationship partner may want to continue to date you while seeing other people, but he or she won't say that because you might not agree to sleep with him or her in that arrangement. Women are territorial once they have made love to someone; they like to know they belong to just that one man. But the two people should be adult enough to say, "Look, I like you, but I am seeing other people. Let's continue to date."

Of course, that doesn't mean you have to have a sexual relationship, but you can continue to get to know each other. The dating process cultivates the idea of being and living in love. When the sexual aspect is initiated, however, things can get complicated. Dating should be just dating. The terms of any relationship should be clearly defined by the two parties involved. Make the relationship you are in be worth your while. But if you are not ready for a serious relationship, simply let people know you are dating.

Have a plan in place to protect your best interests until you understand where the relationship is headed. This book will help explain some things you can do to protect yourself while building a healthy foundation to love. The best plan is developed when you know what you want from a relationship, and you are in touch with your inner self. The plan should revolve around you and what's best for you and what results you want from the relationship. Let's face it: when you meet someone, nine times out of ten you are not the only person that *someone* is dating. This is a common mistake that people make— particularly, women. There is hardly a man or woman on this earth who is not in some type of relationship—maybe with as many as two or three other people. People enjoy sharing a connection with other people so the odds of someone being completely single are slim to none. Going into a relationship with this mind-set can be liberating. It allows you to be more realistic and practical in your expectations of the outcome of the relationship.

However, just because someone may be in a relationship with others doesn't mean he or she won't cultivate an exclusive relationship with you. It is all about the connection we make with people and how they make us feel. Being aware that you are a creature of love, will allow you to connect with a person on whatever level the universe meant for you to connect without the burden of wondering if this person is the one. Love will happen if it supposed to.

When preparing to date, you must be the best *you* that you can be. We will discuss measures you can evaluate to determine if you are the best form of yourself, while lending space to another person to compliment your being. You need to access your skills, strengths, and weaknesses so that you can be an asset to the relationship. Examining yourself is a hard thing to do because it is hard to admit you are not perfect, but it's actually a refreshing experience. It may even be fun to make a list of the quirky things you do that you would like to change.

This book will explore all the areas of one's life that need to be examined while they are looking for love and understanding you are the love you want to see in others. This book will allow you to take a deeper look at yourself and possibly decide on some things you could change to improve who you are. The main theme throughout this book is knowing love happens. You don't have to create love because it already exists. The benefits of altering some things about one's self could help cultivate a healthier relationship with people in your life with and ultimately, cultivate the romance you always dreamed of.

CHAPTER I

Why We Love

It always saddens me to see someone struggling in a relationship because they are looking for the other person to be their savior. Sometimes we discredit a person or relationship based on the fact they can't fill every void in our life. Love is sometimes mistaken as a co-dependent relationship shared between two people. Someone can miss finding love because they are looking for someone to fill an emptiness. This is not possible. We don't really understand why we love. There isn't one person who can be your savior; no individual is equipped with the tools to give someone everything he or she needs. You should come into the relationship with everything you need, physically, mentally, and emotionally; the other person should simply compliment your existence.

Two important things you need before entering any relationship is Love and Happiness. Marvin Gaye said it best. Love and Happiness are what make you who you are. We love because it makes us happy and we are happy when we love. Loving someone is not about making them complete or filling in the gaps. We love because it is a natural process shared between two souls.

If you are in a relationship and don't feel fulfilled or happy, evaluate why you feel that way. Were you unhappy before the relationship started? If so, how do you expect this unknowing person to correct that? Is the relationship depleting your happiness? Is it because your partner is cruel to you, says things that hurt your feelings, or compares you to his or her ex? Next, decide what you are going to do about it. If you had bad feelings prior to the relationship, it easy to carry these feelings into the relationship and blame this person as the root to your bad feelings. Truthfully, you manifested these feelings into existence and the other person is simply returning the energy you give to them.

It is very important to ensure we are at a state of happiness because it will set the tone for our relationships. It is our responsibility and mission as we travel this life's dimension to uncover the essence of our happiness. We should seek the center of being that exudes the expression of happiness and express this feeling daily. The person you choose to share this experience with will give to you what he receives from you. If you exude happiness you will receive happiness. If you exude joy you will receive joy. Ant the opposite is true. If you project misery, you will receive misery.

Happiness is an experience; it is not an emotion (Acacia Parks, 2017). There is no material item that can replace this experience. Ever wonder why rich people still aren't happy? The reason is because their daily experience in life isn't a pleasant one. Happiness is defined by researchers as a combination of how satisfied we are with life and how good we feel on day to day basis. (Acacia Parks, 2017). We have the power to make ourselves happy. It is not in the hands of our mate, family, or friends. If you have a relationship with the Creator of the Universe, you have the complete capability to be happy independent of a relationship with someone.

Most marriages are centered on the idea of happily ever after, without taking into consideration all the work it takes to obtain this obscure outcome. What does *happily ever after* really mean? Who's responsible for making this happen?

The 2004 movie *The Notebook* famously tells of a woman who suffers from dementia and her husband who reads their story to her to remind her of her life. This is one of my favorite movies and I learned the movie is based on a romance novel by Nicholas Sparks, and there are real examples of this type love in our society. Jack and Phyllis Potter are the real British version of the "Notebook". In his early nineties, Jack Potter refuses to let the love of his life slip away to the evil disease of dementia. Jack started keeping a journal when he was a child, and he kept up the practice his entire life. On October 4, 1941, Jack met Phyllis and his diary captured their romance. It was almost love and first site as he wrote: "Very nice evening. Danced with a very nice girl. I hope I see her again." Sixteen months after the first encounter, the two were married. They lived in Kent, England, for over half a century. The dementia didn't discourage Jack. He visits her every day. And every day, he reads to her from his diaries. He reminds her of their family and pets with photographs. Through everything, Phyllis hasn't forgotten how much she loves Jack. Sharing the stories of their memories and pictures of their story was the reminder of why they loved each other. They have now been married for seventy years. (Harlow, 2014)

This story is a very sweet and enduring story, but we don't know all the ins and out of their past seventy years. I am sure there are a lot of up and downs that happened through the years but knowing why you love someone will outweigh a negative circumstance. Moreover, knowing how to be happy through difficult times is even more important.

In the movie Notebook, Allie almost marries another man, who society says was more suited for her. Noah, had another girlfriend when Allie came to visit. Allie realized, in the movie, she couldn't be without Noah. Noah realized he didn't want to be without Allie. They made a conscious decision to choose what made them happy – it wasn't just love, it was the experience they shared with the other person that surged their happiness. The experience they shared with the other person increased their happiness. I am sure they loved each other but I am sure they also loved and cared about the other person they were with as well. But, sometimes, the experience you share with another person is more fulfilling because it increases your level of happiness. You can spend seventy years with someone because you like the experience and space you share with them.

Now imagine the opposite; if you don't know what happiness feels like or don't experience it regularly, you would not know to make the choice Allie and Noah made in the movie. For this reason, people choose a person for what they think the person can be or what the person says they can be instead of choosing the experience.

The happy ever after term is very misleading. It leads one to think it is our mates' responsibility to make us happy. That can't be, because we should embody our happiness prior to meeting our mate. The relationship we share with our significant other may broaden the scope of our happiness, but it can't define it. Trying to make someone happy everyday can cause relationship fatigue and hind the things you initially like about that person.

I had to tell my husband how exhausting it was to constantly try to show him how much I loved him everyday. For a while it seemed like we started the love process all over again when woke up. I begin to experience relationship fatigue. I was tired of being in the relationship because any mistake I made, or mistake he made caused him to question our love. I had a very serious conversation with my husband and explained to him that I loved him because I love God not because he deserved love. I also explained that my love is constant and just because he is having a bad day or experiencing negative feelings about a situation, shouldn't cause him to feel my love was depleted. I don't think he understood at first – especially when I told him, I don't love him because he deserves it. As a matter of fact, he was furious when I told him that. But, as time went on I showed him what I was talking about. No man deserves love, we all make mistakes, but love is patient, kind and true. Mistakes shouldn't determine the amount of love you have for someone. If you are going to love them, then just love them.

I showed my husband how I love by the things I do; like organize his sock drawer, or hang up his clothes, or cook him a red velvet cake because it is his favorite are all manifestations of my love. I do those things because I am choosing to show my love. I chose to enjoy our experience. Times get bad, and there have been some bad times, but I chose to focus on the good and not the bad. I chose my happiness. It took my a while and some self-reflection to realize this point, but it was liberating when I did.

Being in love doesn't mean you will adore every second you spend with someone but it does mean you can have compassion and consideration for the other person's experience. Learning to chose happiness through bad times will increase the connection you share with someone and leads back to why you love them.

Happiness is a state of being we must train ourselves to achieve. Science suggest happiness is a complex combination of genes and day to day activities, and we have the power to increase our happiness by choosing our thoughts, behaviors, and actions (Acacia Parks, 2017). Therefore, we are the only ones who can control our happy state.

To help determine what areas may need a boost to improve our happiness we should assess our *core self,* the personality traits that encompass the subconscious. This is the part of us that lies dormant and is often not realized. According to psychotherapist Rachel Eddins, "Core self is your true self, or most authentic self." It is our "inner wisdom, inner nurturer, wise self, feeling self, inner voice." It is our values and personality, she said. The core self is our essence—our intuition. It is vital to connect to our core, so we can draw the same essence and quality from our potential mates. This step will help establish and determine how centered we are and what areas of our inner beings need improvement; it also will help us figure out which aspects of our beings we want to keep intact which will in turn cause us to be happier people. Eddins teaches why you should uncover your core beliefs. Uncovering, your core beliefs can help identify why you keep repeating patterns or behaviors in your life. Maybe you find yourself always drawing a toxic or negative relationship in your life or maybe your mate always tends to cheat on you. There may be some core beliefs in your inner being that cause you to repeat these actions, for example you feel the world is unsafe, or you feel all men cheat. By evaluating the core of your being you will begin to understand the connection between your beliefs and your feelings and ultimately be able to obtain a healthy level of happiness (Rachel Eddins, 2014). We draw people into our lives. If you are drawing negative relationships in your life; you are exuding those negatives traits. You may be unaware you are releasing these negative feelings, but your relationship patterns reveal the truth.

Every action and emotion we have is centered on a feeling. That feeling is centered on a belief and what you value. It is our job to access the validity of our beliefs. Our beliefs and values always resonate in our day to day life; the kind of job we have, the way we dress, the way we wear our hair; all these things are cultivated by our beliefs. What a person believes to be true a valid concept, shapes how they live their life and react others. There doesn't have to be empirical evidence the belief is true, but the fact that a person has a faith that the concept is so serves as their point of validity. For example, some people believe going to church will increase their chances of going to heaven. There is no solid proof that this concept is so but being a raised in a church environment and being taught that going to church is the right thing to do, serves as your source of validity. This belief then turns into something you value. You place value in something because you believe it to be true. Our values are the things that are important to us. Beliefs and values shape our feelings and drive our emotion. The diagram below shows the sequence of emotions.

Beliefs and values can have a direct effect on our ability to express love and be happy. . If we go backwards up the diagram and we can determine how people derive at an emotion. I believe, we don't love based on what we believe, we love based on our feelings. We skip two very important steps when we are looking for love. There are various reasons why we skip these steps but we typically to. We go straight for the feeling and emotion.

For example, a man may believe a woman should cook for him daily because that was his experience as a child. His belief in this quality cause this attribute to hold value in his life. Because a woman doesn't cook for him he may become angry; this angry causes him to hit her. Even though he loves this woman very much the anger about her not cooking cause a negative feeling. It may be a feeling he is not capable of dealing with.

If he chose love based on his belief, he would have married someone who cooks but that is not in our normal pattern. We typically marry based on the feeling and experience. But our beliefs, which generate a separate feeling, can affect our love. Therefore, a man who beats his wife can say "Yes I love my wife." He really does love her, but a belief and overpowering feeling of emotion causes a negative action leaving him powerless to express love in a heartfelt, gentler, manner. But the true issue is his belief. His rigid belief is causing a negative impact on his relationship. Some of our beliefs and values are so firm, it can cause you a relationship.

Some of our beliefs have been taught to us and some have been adopted from your environment. Where ever the belief comes from; we must evaluate the beliefs to assess their validity in our life cycle and determine how it may be affecting our ability to be happy and express love in a positive way. If a person doesn't grow up seeing positive displays of affection; they will not have the skills to display love in a positive way. Moreover, their core being is not in a state of bliss and peace; their ego has taken the front seat to their soul, so the person may not have a positive reservoir within themselves to draw positive energy. A belief should be tested and reaffirmed. You may find there are a lot of beliefs you can dispose of or redefine if it inhibiting you from expressing love in it's purest form.

A lot of people deal with the issue of expressing love. They believe love expressions leave them vulnerable and they fear they will not get the expression in return. Our ego says we can't show how we feel because it will make you appear week. The opposite is true, love is strength. We are designed to love. Removing the expectation of receiving something in return and suppressing the ego will free one to love as their heart leads. Even though it is easier to love when there is no threat of rejection, like holding a newborn baby, we must learn to love through the awkwardness and probability of rejection.

Abraham Maslow proposed the Maslow hierarchy of needs in his 1943 research paper "A Theory of Human Motivation." In this paper, Maslow explains all the things humans need for fundamental development and one of the items on the hierarchy is love and belonging. He defines this need as humans needing to feel a sense of belonging (Maslow, 1943). Love is being apart of someone. When we feel love, we feel connected and drawn to a person. Maslow points out this need is especially strong in childhood (Maslow, 1943). Imagine as a child never receiving the feeling of love or belonging. Their will be a huge emotional gap. It is our human nature to love. This is how some people end up feeling someone can be their savior. There is such a huge void in their life and they believe the only way it can be filled is by another person. The sense of love and belonging is just that strong.

We love because we must. We should share a spiritual and inner connection with someone. Love and happiness make us who we are, and relationships allow us to express these feelings.

CHAPTER 2

Love happens in phases. When we initially meet someone, we normally experience the feeling of infatuation. The infatuation phase is a very complicated time because this is oftentimes, mistake for love. But research suggest the infatuation phase lasts about two years, and after that, love takes over.

The first phase of love is the romance. The romantic phase is driven by estrogen and testosterone. There is strong physical attraction, and the stage is set for emotional attachment. This phase of love is filled with pleasure and good feelings. You feel your mate is perfect for you. It is also noted during this time, there is high sexual energy.

As we get older and more mature, we have the desire to find the "right one." We believe the right one is the one that will give us the love we so desperately want and need. I believe most people experience the desire to get married for the sense of belonging represented on Maslow's Hierarchy of needs, and not necessary for the commitment that comes along with it. People want to feel connected to someone in an intimate way and feel marriage is the best way to achieve this level of love and connection. Most people may not, actively, be looking for love but looking for companionship and are typically teetering on the romance phase of love. We like the idea of being with someone and feeling head over heals in love. This is when the relationship is fresh and new. During this phase of my relationship with my husband, I could just come home from work and just lay on the couch in his arms. Time almost stood still as I laid on his chest.

During phase one people will ignore the red flags that they later must deal with phase two. Phase is a blinding phase and we want what our hormones tell us we need. When a person is attractive to you it sets the hormones in motion. We are bombarded with these feelings. Phenyleteylamine is a hormone that is called the molecule of love because it is the leader in producing these feelings (John Gottman, The Three Phases of Love, 2014).

The second phase of love is physical attraction and power struggle. During this phase the hormones dopamine, norepinephrine, and serotonin are racing through your body. You become more realistic, and you and your partner may argue more. Partners are struggling to build trust (John Gottman, The Three Phase of Love, 2014). Infatuation is wearing off, and strong emotional attachment has set in. We want to be around this person more and more, but conflicts arise more during this phase.

Dopamine is a hormone that drives motivations, addictions attention and desire. When this hormone is released it produces a feeling of happiness (Zbigniew Chmielewski, 2016). This happiness feeling is addictive and drives us deeper into the relationship. We become fully invested in the relationship. This phase is sometimes referred to as the honeymoon phase. This phase typically lasts a few months up to two years (Zbigniew Chmielewski, 2016).

The third phase of love is emotional attachment and unconditional love. During this phase, a mature love relationship develops, and you become more committed to your mate. You commit to a partnership and maybe even to having children. The hormone oxytocin and vasopressin are more dominant. These hormones play a role in social and reproductive features. Oxytocin is referred to as the love hormone because it correlates a bond between humans based on touch. Kissing, hugging and sex enhance the bond between two people during this phase of love (Zbigniew Chmielewski, 2016).

During the third phase of love, a person becomes aware of both positive and negative traits. You will argue more severely and may decide to commit to each more intensely or call it quits. The sense of power needs to be distributed fairly. This phase is about making a love last a lifetime and slowly nurturing a behavior (John Gottman, The Three Phase of Love, 2014). For me, this phase has been intense. After having children, our commitment to each other was heightened. We felt like we have to get this right because we have small children watching and depending on us. We both get emotionally drained easier and are often exhausted. The good thing is, we can see the silver lining. We plan how our children's future will be and how our life will be after they are grown. The work comes in remembering to spend time with the mate because the raising of children often seems all consuming. I am assured because I know our goals are aligned and we want the same thing for our family.

The phases of love can vary, and the outcome can be unpredictable. There are outside forces that can influence the evolution of the relationship. If a couple have children, this could potentially affect the phases of love. However, it is affected, the phases of love happen and sometimes the relationship grows stronger and sometimes it doesn't last.

We are all connected to each other. When we look for love, we say we want to find our soul mate. When we are single, we say, "I am looking for my soul mate." But is there just one soul mate in this wide world for you? Absolutely not! All of our souls are connected because we are all connected to God. Soul mates can be anyone—relatives, friends, coworkers, or significant others. Soul mate relationships are designed to make you better as a person, awaken you, and discover your true self. The soul mate is simply someone who aligns with your soul and allows your soul to ascend to a higher level of consciousness. However, your soul may have a better connection with another soul than another.

You meet someone at the coffee shop, make eye contact, and exchange a few kind words. You may run into that person again at the park. This time, he or she gets your phone number. The conversation goes well. As things move to friendship, you immediately start the checklist to see why you should not talk to this person or have him or her as a friend. That is completely wrong. This person you met at the coffee shop may not be your life partner or he or she could be, but this person could very well be a soul mate who will put you on the avenue to meeting your destiny. But since we are so smart, thinking everyone is out to get us, and we know exactly what we need, we weed out people who were designed to be there all along and were meant to carry us to the next level of our cosmic journeys.

The choice, however, is yours. You may have had so many bad relationships that you think it is impossible to find a good guy, but that is far from the truth. Each encounter is independent, and it is your job to take a lesson from the experience. If you continue to make the same mistake over and over again in dating, you aren't in tune with your spirit and soul enough to realize who complements your positives and who brings out your negatives. The spirit world sends us soul mates throughout life who can shape and strengthen us as individuals. Soul mates are the people who meet the following points:

- You may feel a deep connections to them, almost like you have known them before.
- You experience déjà vu moments with them.
- You have similar childhoods.
- Your relationship with them can move from extreme highs to extreme lows.
- You feel in sync with them, even when you are not together.
- Your relationship is emotional and can bring things out of you that you didn't know existed.
- Your relationship may not last forever, but the love is always there.

Soul mates have certain effects on your life because their purpose is to move you into higher dimensions. It's up to you to take the challenge and accept the experience for what it is. Soul mates may not travel into your future, but you will always feel their presence in your life.

We have the capability to connect with everyone spiritually, and the bond is stronger with some more than with others. If there isn't a strong bond initially, then the relationship may not last. But the great thing about that is, it is okay. Relationships teach us something and sometimes we encounter people that are supposed to teach us something on life's journey that will take us to a higher spiritual level. At the end of the day, it is about the journey. It is about the relationships that make us smarter, wiser and more spiritually grounded. It is about the relationships that help us define our beliefs and values and get us more in tune with the messages being sent from the Creator. We are divine beings placed on earth to elevate our spiritual existence. Relationships can help us with this. Every soul has a mate and all souls share similarities because they are connected to the creator. We are all more alike than different.

Once a guy was in love with a girl. She wasn't the most beautiful, but for him, she was everything. He dreamed about her, about spending the rest of his life with her. His friends told him, "Why do you dream so much about her when you don't even know if she loves you? First tell her your feelings and find out if she likes you."

He felt that was the right way. The girl knew from the beginning that this guy loved her. One day when he proposed, she told him no. His friends thought he would overdose on alcohol or drugs and would ruin his life. To their surprise, her rejection didn't depress him.

When his friends asked him why he wasn't sad, he replied, "Why should I feel sad? I lost one who never loved me, and she lost the one who really loved and cared for her."

Moral: True love is hard to get. Appreciate the honesty and simplicity of love.

CHAPTER 3

Marriage Isn't Love

Nowadays, the institution of marriage has been placed in a negative light. People may be losing faith in marriage because of the high divorce rate, but people are not losing faith in love, which seems slightly contradictory. How could this be? People believe in love but not marriage.

It is easy to understand because marriage isn't love. Marriage is a legal union of two people, created by God, that has been happening since the dawn of time. It is an agreement to share the responsibilities of raising a family and to have companionship. In the Bible, God made Eve, so Adam wouldn't be alone. It is easier to understand marriage, when you look at this way. Marriage isn't so complicated, really, just misunderstood.

According to a 2013 Pew Research study, 88 percent of Americans cited love as their reason for getting married. Marriage may be facing a difficult phase, but people still want love. If people still want love, then why don't they want the marriage? It may have something to do with the amount of work required to sustain a marriage.

There are quite a few interesting statistics about marriages that make people feel marriage is not worth the hassle. According to NakedLaw.com, a website written by technology lawyers, someone gets a divorce every ten to thirteen seconds, and those who marry between the ages of twenty and twenty-four have the highest divorce rates; it also claims that adults who didn't attend college and have low household incomes are likely to be divorced at a rate of 20 percent. However, despite all the negative statistics, things recently have begun to look up for marriage. The decade with the highest divorce rate was from the 1970s to the 1980s. According to the *Huffington Post*, the fact that people are now marrying late in life, resulting in more mature marriages, has helped the marriage success rates go up in recent years. Interestingly, the median age for marriages in the 1950s was twenty-three; as of 2004, it rose to age twenty-seven. As of 2013, a recent study found the average age for marriage to be twenty-seven for women and twenty-nine for men. (Lenz, 2016) This is likely because people are accomplishing their educational and career goals before they get married. Pew Research Center confirms marriage is losing relevance among Americans to other arrangement like cohabitation (Cohn, 2011). Surprisingly, the success rate in America for marriage is increasing. Research has found that divorce rates peak in the 1980s at a staggering 40% but has steadily declined since. According to statistics from the National Survey of Family Growth, the probability of the first marriage lasting a decade is 68% for women and 70% for men. Since 1990, roughly 75 percent of those who married reportedly reach their fifteen-year anniversaries (Jacoby, 2017). Wouldn't you agree that's pretty good?

The next marital statistic that frightens people is the "seven-year itch." People don't want to be married to someone who cheats. It is a terrifying predicament, but many couples go through it. I did, and the marriage survived. Statistics show that on average, couples who break up do so upon seven years of marriage. There is something about seven years that causes the marriage to go haywire. There's an inclination to become unfaithful and to lose interest in your spouse after seven years. Seven years may not seem like a long time, but a lot of things can happen in seven years.

Rudolf Steiner, an Australian philosopher and teacher, created a theory of development based on a seven-year cycle that affects our bodies and is associated with astrology. This development theory may explain why people become disinterested in their marriages after seven years. According to Steiner's theory, humans experience physical and mental changes every seven years. These changes are beyond our control and are affected by the universe. The first seven years of life are associated with the moon. During this time, psychic forces are working to transform the body of the child from one that was inherited from the parents to the full personality of the child. The second seven years are associated with Mercury. Currently, the child's imagination and feeling of life take center stage. The third seven years are associated with Venus. During this time the higher mind of the adolescent takes root, and his or her psychic development can be disturbed by the strong impulses of puberty. The next three seven-year periods (from twenty-one to forty-two years old) are associated with Mars, when the soul takes the opportunity to achieve a higher state of consciousness called the *spirit self* (Armstrong, 2012)

Steiner's theory suggests that with these different evolutional changes taking place in the body and soul, your point of view changes, which can lead to a change in the way you feel for your spouse. I don't know if this is true, but the research is interesting and reiterates how hard you must work to sustain a marriage and family. Not only must you fight against people who will try to degrade the marriage but also, against outside forces in the universe (Armstrong, 2012). Marriage is sacred and blessed by God, so it is understandable that demonic forces will rise against a marriage.

As individuals grow older, they mature and become more connected to their inner selves (their souls and spirits), which propels them to reach for higher aspirations. Our constant self-evolution over time pushes us to higher callings. Sometimes couples say they have outgrown each other, or they no longer share common interests. This development in our life cycles could cause two people to grow apart if they don't work to stay connected (Armstrong, 2012).

In 1999, a study by Dr. Larry A. Kurdek, who was a psychology professor at Wright State University, established the legitimacy of possibly both a four- and a seven-year itch. His research demonstrated that couples often began their marriages with a certain level of marriage integrity and quality, but it appeared to decrease twice: once rather steeply over the first four years and again after about seven years. His study also showed that couples with children experienced a more rapid decline in the quality of marriage. Some research even suggests there is a four-, seven-, and twelve-year itch (Nagy, 2013). So no matter how someone may feel about marriage, it is truly difficult for people to stay married.

In choosing the right mate, you cut down on the anxiety you may face later in your marriage, after having children and dealing with financial responsibilities. Having the right mate, means you have someone who helps balance the stress. No person should feel like he or she is carrying all the responsibility in the marriage on his or her shoulders. These responsibilities are meant to be shared. However, it's human nature to make mistakes and overlook things. We may feel we are carrying our share of the load, while our spouses may feel we are not. This is when we should have a conversation about how we feel and come to a loving understanding.

Statistics seem mixed, but probably one in five married couples you know are either divorced or experiencing marital problems instead of marital bliss. No wonder marriage has a negative image. So where does the happily-ever-after take over? Who is responsible for this happiness?

It's obvious that couples must put in extra effort every day to sustain their marriages. People put so much emphasis on the wedding, giving little or no thought to how much work they need to put into the actual marriage. It takes some people an entire year to plan a wedding, an event that will last one day, but they won't put any work or planning into the success of their marriages. If a one-day event requires a year's worth of preparation, how much preparation and work do you think you need for something that is supposed to last the rest of your life?

Each stage of your life prior to marriage is important to building a healthy foundation for your core self and ultimately your marriage. The key attributes self-dependence, self-realization, commitment, and motivation are fundamental in helping secure a healthy balance in love and marriage. These three attributes are essential in helping one determine what could be helping or hindering their love life.

Recognizing whether you are truly ready for marriage requires an honest and sincere frame of mind. I met my husband as I was leaving work one day. There were some apartments near where I was parked, and he was standing on the terrace of the apartments. As I strolled to my car, I glanced up and saw him—a complete stranger—waving at me as if he knew me. I kind threw my hand up in a quick greeting but hurried to my car. A few days later as I was leaving work, he drove past me in his truck. He held up one finger, indicating I should stop.

I thought, *Oh, gosh, who is this guy?* But I waited for him as he pulled up and parked. He got out of his truck and approached me with his hand out to shake my hand. I saw two shiny gold teeth in the front of his mouth and a huge tattoo on the arm that was extended to me. Immediately I realized he was not my type.

He said, "Hi, my name is Drudon." I said hello. Then there was a moment of silence as he took off his sunglasses, which seemed to happen in slow motion, like in the movies. I couldn't wait for the shades to come off, so I could see his eyes; I wanted to see his eyes. When the shades finally came off and I could see his face, I realized this man was attractive—I mean *really* attractive, and those eyes were a dream. He had the most adorable slanted eyes rimmed with long dark eyelashes. I loved those eyes. Although I can't remember, I must have been smiling from ear to ear. I do remember that I was smiling on the inside because he looked good to me. He said a few more words, and I went on my way.

We ran into each other a few more times after that, and I eventually gave him my house phone number but not my cell phone number because I had a boyfriend. (Remember what I said earlier—when you meet someone, it is almost a guarantee he or she is involved with someone else?) He called me a couple of times, but I played too hard to get, which was my style. I was occupied with my boyfriend and just occupied with life in general. Besides, it seemed that we were from two different worlds, even though there was something about him I liked.

One day, I checked my answering machine, and he'd left a distinct message: "Hey, this is Drudon. You never answer the phone, so I guess that means you don't want me to call, so I won't call you anymore."

Oh no! I thought. *I better call this guy back because he was fine.* When I returned his call, we stayed on the phone for hours. Talking to him was like talking to a long-lost friend. He kept me laughing. His personality was so adorable to me. After our initial conversation, I couldn't get him off my mind. Talking to him was so refreshing.

At this point in my life, I was super content and overjoyed with my circumstances. I had just graduated college and had a job, my own apartment, a cool boyfriend, and a gang of friends. I was in relaxation mode and enjoying the fruits of my labor. Life was great! I was fairly self-dependent. When I met Lee aka Duron (I learned his real name months later), I had no idea he would be the guy I would marry. I'd figured I would marry the guy I was currently in a relationship with. We had been together four years, and I thought we had a lot in common. We both attended Ole Miss together and had shared a lot of fun times and created memories.

I meet so many young women who, at the age of twenty-three, are living their lives for everybody but themselves. Twenty-three is a young age when a person is trying to figure everything out and decide what really makes him or her happy. This can be really great time in life because you are young, and you feel invincible. You feel as if nothing in the world can hurt you. It is a great time to explore the world and learn about you. This may not be the best time to decide to be in a committed relationship, but this is definitely an important time in your life. Self-dependence and self-reliance is the virtue of supporting yourself and learning what you need and who you are. Self- dependence is relying on your own strength and no one else's. Physical and emotional self-dependence is a freeing experience because is helps you have a healthy outlook on life.

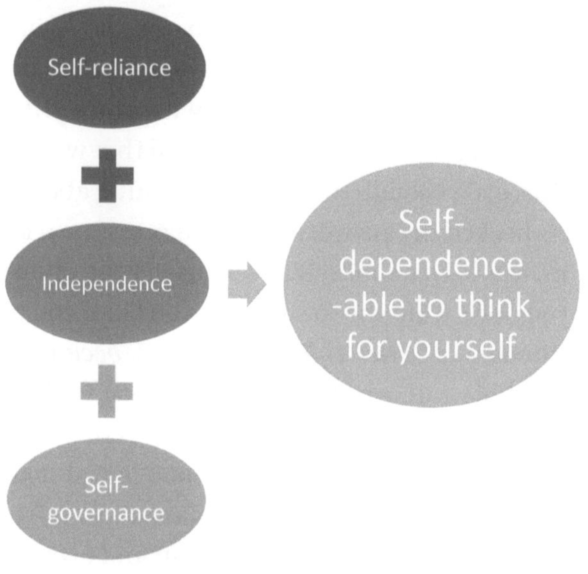

Situations happen in life that will take you away from the process of getting to know your trust self, such as an unplanned pregnancy or loss of a loved one. These obstacles make it harder but not impossible to learn how to be independent. If you can prevent an unplanned pregnancy, you should. Your life deserves your commitment to the process of fulfilling your purpose. Don't let something like an unplanned pregnancy deter you from your dreams. Plan your life accordingly.

The MTV show *Teen Mom* depicts the ups and downs of unplanned pregnancy. It shows the transition from puberty to motherhood. That show is a demonstration of how life sometimes gets in the way. I find it so funny that the teenage couple portrayed is always so in love before the baby comes into the picture. Then the boy realizes he wants to keep his life the same and have fun while the girl transitions to a higher calling of motherhood. The shift often causes resentment, and the resentment turns into frustration. The frustration turns into anger. Before you know it, the two are fighting over who bought the last pack of diapers, when they are angry over the life transition that has left them feeling alone and overwhelmed.

They may lose some of their close friends because the friendships become awkward. But since the teens lacks the ability to be self-dependent, the underlying issues are not properly addressed. These feelings lead to extreme anxiety and ultimately avoidance. The teen avoids the situation completely because dealing with is causes to much anxiety. This upheaval mostly leads to a nasty breakup. Therefore, it is extremely important to get to know yourself as an individual before you throw other people and innocent lives in the mix. Two unhappy people can't make a happily-ever-after. When a girl is young, she should make a conscious effort to better understand herself and not deal with the stress of raising a child or trying to make a "baby daddy" grow up and be a man. It takes her away from her self-dependence experience.

HelloBeautiful.com, a pop culture website that celebrates "millennial women of color," says the experience of being independent is important for five reasons:

1. Independence allows you to take control of your destiny. Your destiny is in line with your purpose in life. You are able to

become your own leader, and you can make your own rules, with aspirations of reaching your destiny. Independence gives you the platform to manifest the dreams you have for life. Any goal you want to achieve is outlined during your independence.

2. Independence helps boost self-confidence. You become able to believe in your ability to take care of yourself, and you may even discover that you are pretty good at it. Self-confidence is important because it's the driving force behind everything you do. If you are sure of yourself, you will want the best for yourself.
3. Independence allows you to gain perspective on your life. You get to view your life from the sidelines, so to speak, and you can critique yourself. Operating independently allows you to see situations as they happen in a clearer light. You will have a better understanding of where you are and where you want to go.
4. You will rely on yourself for all your needs (self-reliance). Once you become an adult, you should allow yourself the opportunity to become comfortable relying on yourself and becoming your own fabulous self.
5. You will learn to be yourself, which will help you to trust, believe, and love yourself.

These five key attributes allow you to learn your strengths and weaknesses and, more important, you will learn self-governing. For example, "I do not like it when_______________." Or "When I see this, it makes me feel _______________." Self-governance allows you to fill in these blanks and set guidelines on how people can treat you. Some people are born with a clearer instinct to display self-governance, while others may have to practice it, but whatever the case, self-governance is required to build a healthy relationship with yourself and ultimately a healthy foundation to deal with others. You have to teach people how to treat you, and you cannot do this until you know how to treat yourself.

Respect, embrace, and trust your feelings during your independence. The best time to process feelings and emotions, I believe, is when you are alone. When you are by yourself in a quiet room or space, you can become connected to your feelings and emotions and begin to understand yourself. If your gut tells you the way someone is speaking to you is offensive, then trust this feeling. This is what makes you an individual. Trust your feelings, and learn how to process them. We often learn how to *feel* based on people's reactions. This makes us lose our individuality, and we learn not to trust ourselves. We wait for someone's response before we react, secretly wanting the person's approval. This is the opposite of what we should do. We should practice rationalizing our feelings. It may help to talk with someone you trust, such as a very close friend. Discuss your feelings with that person. Sometimes saying things out loud helps to clarify feelings.

If we don't learn how to properly process our feelings, it may lead to insecurity and the feeling of wanting to be accepted by others. But this insecurity can be overcome. Learn that it is okay to feel the way you feel, but be able to explain or understand why you feel that way. It is self-governance and trust that gives us the backbone we need in a relationship. Self-governance doesn't have anything to do with other people; it's all about you. When you effectively display self-governance, which simply means you are not controlled by outside forces, you can build relationships with boundaries and requirements. (More on that later.)

I married a ladies' man—a man who loves women and who women love. To be with someone with such a personality requires a strong backbone and strong identity—but any relationship does, for that matter. When you are completely and utterly in love with yourself, life can happen. This means you can consciously allow things to happen in life without feeling like a prisoner to what the outcome may be. You don't go through life planning for something bad to happen, but if it does, you know it's not the end of the world. I didn't hold it against my husband because he had that type of past, but if he wanted to be with me, there were certain things he had to do. More importantly, if the relationship didn't work out, I knew it wouldn't be the end of the world.

For example, when we hung out together, I never portrayed myself as being desperate. I exuded self-confidence, and I let life happen. I didn't get paranoid every time his phone rang or question him about who had called. It just wasn't that big of a deal (until we became exclusive, which came years later). Lee and I both had significant others, but we did hang out together. We developed a friendship. We had no idea we would get married.

.Allow yourself to be open to the experiences that are going on around you, whether the experiences are good or bad. Allow yourself to feel what is going on. If the experience is bad, then you will learn that you don't want that feeling again, and you will take the proper steps to avoid that feeling. All feelings and actions in relationships can start and end with you. You must learn to put your feelings in check and process them accordingly.

I remember when I was younger, around eighteen years old, it was extremely difficult for me to go places by myself. For example, just an outing to the mall felt awkward if I was alone. I didn't want to experience that awkwardness, and I was too insecure and unaccustomed to my own company. But now that I'm older, a trip to the mall by myself sounds like a vacation—it's a wonderful thing! I have grown and matured.

Getting to know yourself and maturing brings about a certain level of confidence. As you get older, you must practice techniques that allow you to expand and mature as an individual. Hang out with people who are different from you. Read autobiographies on different people's journeys. Listen more than you talk, and don't assume you know everything. Be slow to anger—anger gets in the way of the learning experience. You can learn something from every person you meet.

Webster's defines self-realization as "the theory that the highest good for man consists in realizing or fulfilling himself, usually on the assumption that he has certain inborn abilities constituting his real or ideal self." Self-awareness is another way to describe this trait. Anadi Teaching is a revelation of supreme understanding. Anadi is a spiritual teacher, who, throughout his life, has perfected the experience of connecting to your inner self. Anadi explains self-realization as being completely aware of yourself. Truly practicing and understanding this concept helps you see that self-realization is the absence of ego and the presence of your true self. Does anyone take the time to discover his or her true self? It is sometimes easier to present an ego to people because it makes us seem tough and relatable. At the end of the day, we just want people to like us. It seems scary to be different, but it doesn't have to be.

According to Anadi Teaching, self-realization is a spiritual and philosophical concept—being able to fully understand the intricacies of the various dimensions of self that we are realizing (Anadi, 2017). As we grow, we are to become in tune with who we are destined to be. We should seek a connection with our spirits and souls. We should make a genuine effort to be in tune with who we are. This realization of self is a state of wholeness that manifests through the awakening of three levels of our existence: personal, individual, and universal. We must understand that these three elements shape our human experience bringing us in alignment with who you are.

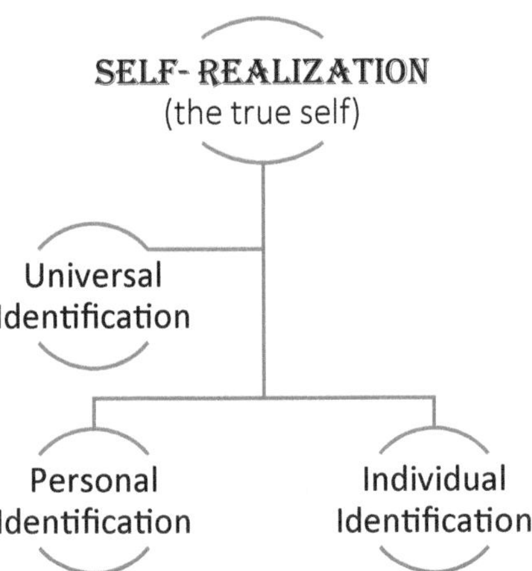

Personal realization is the evolution of me. Our "me" is our child, our true friend and life companion, our beloved. It is our highest responsibility to honor it and serve with all our existence. One of the ways our "me" hopes to bridge itself with creation is by seeking love and emotional fulfillment. We all remember what we felt like as children—our innocence and desire to be loved and how it felt when we received love from a parent or grandparent. The collective mind constantly creates stories of love or great sacrifice. This is seen in our dreams. This is how the body exudes the need for love. Yes, we all require love because it is the greatest feeling emotion of all. Our "me" desires this feeling because it is a chemistry that our body needs like food. Love is life's greatest blessing. Personal self-realization expands to the desire to be pure, honest, and loving. Our "me" wants pure, honest love (Anadi, 2017).

Individual self-realization allows the soul to come into being. One matures toward this concept; it cannot be produced. This is the light of "I am." Individual self-realization involves fusing "me" with "I am" and becoming our deeper selves (Anadi, 2017). This is a deep experience that can be awakening if experienced to it's full compacity. As a girl becomes a woman, although, this concept is mostly natural, she needs to recognize this change is taking place. Individual self-realization is our process of maturing and seeing things on a deeper level as it pertains to us. This process involves developing into who you want to become, but it is influenced by the factors around you and the environment you are in. It is particularly hard sometimes to develop through this phase because there are many outside forces that affect it. We can get lost in this step because our environment may be a negative one that will affect our "I am" in a negative way (Anadi, 2017). This transition sometimes takes longer because people make mistakes and sometimes must rediscover their "I am."

Universal self-realization is the last dimension of self-realization, and it involves awakening the soul. This requires us to evolve into a deeper connection with the Creator. The Creator is our ultimate power source, and to be connected to him is to be empowered (Anadi, 2017). To me, this is the highest form of awakening and the most empowering. We are, actually, always connected to the creator but, to me, this phase requires us to recognize the connection on a more intimate level. This correlation is where we surrender ourselves and our souls to create this deeper connection. The soul is the spiritual part of us. The soul is our divine nature. This connection pushes us to a state of consciousness to know we are just a small speck in the universe, and there is something higher than ourselves. This part of us, too, must mature for us to be the loving, compassionate, and understanding people we need to be in relationships (Anadi, 2017). When we allow the process of self-realization to evolve, and we allow ourselves to become who we are, we can have a deeper connection with ourselves and others.

We may place unrealistic expectations on others especially in a relationship. We choose to believe that they should think and feel as we do. We believe others have the obligation to offer us everything we need. We also believe others should operate at perfection. But if we develop a respect and understanding for the self-realization concept, we will come to understand each person has his or her own journey. Each person's journey has gotten that person to where he or she is. Each person is continually growing and evolving and are not the highest forms of themselves yet.

My husband's father was in a car accident that left him paralyzed from the chest down. My husband was ten years old when this happened. This tragic accident put a lot of responsibility on my husband. He is the middle child of three and is the older son. He had to help take care of his father while his mother was working. The entire dynamic of the family changed drastically, almost overnight. My husband has admitted that he wishes someone would have gotten counseling for him at that point in his life, to deal with all the emotions he was feeling. He was really confused, angry, and hurt. He wasn't equipped with the tools to process such a stream of emotions. As a coping mechanism, my husband learned to suppress his feelings, just to get by. This coping mechanism has followed him his entire life.

When Lee and I were hanging out, he asked me if I would be able to deal with all the children he had. He had seven children. I figured I could deal with it, but I wanted to know why a person would have so many children at such a young age. I was wondering what happened in his life, that would allow him to come to such a decision to continuously have children with different women. During our friendship, I learned that Lee had to grow up fast. He was a good person, but he lacked commitment, understanding, and self-realization. Because of this, he wasn't good with relationships. Because he had to grow up fast, he made decisions he shouldn't have had to make at ten or eleven years old. This stunted some of his psychological development and growth, which should have taken place during his self-realization phase. He chose to embrace his ego instead of embracing his true self. By embracing the ego, he received the attention he needed after feeling hurt and let down as a child. The ego says a person should do what makes them feel good versus doing what is best. Embracing the ego gives a false sense of control and authority; when your life is out of control. The ego is also never satisfied and strives for more power, attention and control.

Everyone doesn't evolve through self-realization at the same rate, and some people don't evolve into their full potential because they don't have the proper tools in place. For example, when you meet your mate, you may be at the universal self-realization phase of your life, and your mate may be struggling with the individual self-realization phase. No two people develop at the same rate or with the same purpose. We must understand this. No one is perfect. and the truth is none of us may completely evolve as we properly should, but we must be able to deal with someone's broken pieces if we want to be with that person. This reminds me of the *Seasons of Life* story.

> There was a man who had four sons. He wanted his sons to learn to not judge things too quickly, so he sent them each on a quest, in turn, to look at a pear tree that was a great distance away.
>
> The first son went in the winter, the second in the spring, the third in summer, and the youngest son in the fall.
>
> When they had all gone and come back, he called them together to describe what they had seen.
>
> The first son said that the tree was ugly, bent, and twisted.
>
> The second son said no, it was covered with green buds and full of promise.
>
> The third son disagreed. He said it was laden with blossoms that smelled so sweet and looked so beautiful. It was the most graceful thing he had ever seen.
>
> The last son disagreed with all of them; he said it was ripe and drooping with fruit, full of life and fulfillment.

> The man then explained to his sons that they were all right because they each had seen but one season in the tree's life.
>
> He told them that they could not judge a tree or a person by only one season and that the essence of who they are—and the pleasure, joy, and love that comes from that life—could only be measured at the end, when all the seasons were up.
>
> If you give up when it's winter, you will miss the promise of spring, the beauty of summer, and the fulfillment of fall.

Don't judge a life by one difficult season. Don't let the pain of one season destroy the joy of all the rest. Apparently, my husband had a difficult season is his life and accumulated a lot of children during that time; but that doesn't have to define the rest of his life if he doesn't want it to.

Everyone has a past full of shattered pieces, and if you really love someone, you can work through it. If you decide you cannot work through those issues, then walk away before you even start to plan that dream wedding. You must realize what you can and can't deal with, while being honest with yourself about the seasons that people's lives go through. Don't assume the situation that makes you uncomfortable will get better or go away, and don't assume it is the worst and things can get no better. Confront the situation head-on, and come to a realistic conclusion. You may not have been able to deal with someone who has seven children, and that is okay, but be fair.

The Christian Broadcasting Network stated in an article on marriage on the website that you must consider someone's past and history when you are dating to get an understanding of what the future may be like with that person. Mark Gungor, a therapist who counsels couples, says a lot of people are not honest with themselves during the dating process. Or they may feel obligated to continue in the relationship even though a lot of red flags arise. The dating process is a time of discovery and analysis. The dating process is glimpse into what a future may look like with this person.

I discovered that Lee had a lot of children, but when I dug deeper into his past, I better understood why this had happened. Even more important, I discovered he wasn't a horrible person, just misguided and maybe even confused. I was comfortable with him as a person and liked him. I liked who he really was inside, and I valued that. At the same time, I had to be honest with myself about how our relationship would work. So as the relationship progressed, I had a conversation with him. I asked him what he would expect from me in regard to his children. I needed to know if he wanted a true "mommy" for them or just a positive role model. I knew I would not be able to be a mother to them because I was only twenty-five at the time and didn't have any children. I was enjoying my life and did not want parenting responsibilities. He told me he just wanted me to treat his children well and that I shouldn't worry about the responsibility; he would handle that. I could live with that. We had an understanding.

It was scary to have that conversation because it could have been the end of the relationship, but it was necessary when that many children are involved. Lee and I did our homework, and it has worked out well.

Self-realization involves being honest with ourselves and the persons we are with. Everyone deserves the truth so he or she can make healthy decisions about his or her life and future. It is extremely difficult for us to admit we are not perfect and have flaws. If Lee had lied to me about how many children he had, then our situation could have been a catastrophe. We tend to want to cover disappointing issues instead of being honest and exposing them. But if we have a clear understanding of who we are and who we desire to be, discussing mistakes from our past shouldn't be scary. I was very impressed how honest he was with me about his children and even more impressed with how well-mannered and nice all of his children were when I met them. If we are uncomfortable discussing issues from our past, it may be because we have not properly dealt with those issues, or we may still be dealing with those issues.

Sometimes people spend their entire lives defending their craziness, instead of just trying to change or admit to it. Yes, change is hard, but it makes for a happier you in the long run. Making healthy changes can help you become a better husband or wife. Don't be afraid to admit there are some things about you that need to change. That doesn't show weakness. It only shows observance and inventory on things that are broken. There is nothing wrong with striving to be a better person. That's what life is about. In 1 Corinthians 13:11, the Bible says, "When I was a child, I spake as a child, but when I became a man I put away childish things." We are expected to grow, change, and evolve; this is what self-realization is all about.

It is a hard to believe that one needs to modify their behavior. But without change, how can we become all that we are designed to be? The first step in changing a behavior is to identify that which needs developing or changing. It may be anger, lying, infidelity, and so on. Once it's identified, put it away. We have to be honest about our weaknesses. How do we put it away? Change the behavior by replacing it with something else. Don't feed the behavior; starve the behavior until it dies. If you love women, and every time you go to the club, you prey on women, stop going to the club. Find something else to do with your Saturday night. For example, plan Saturday night as family night, and take the family bowling. It may not seem fun at first, but you must work on any behavior to make it a habit. If you're a smoker, I assume the first time you smoked a cigarette, it wasn't all that thrilling, but you kept smoking and before you knew it, you had a need for it.

Sometimes we do bad things because there's something about the thrill of it, but release that. That is a trick of the devil. Keep practicing good behavior, and the desire and need to do the bad behavior will die. You must remember—the success of your marriage or relationship depends on you being able to bend when needed.

Troubles arise in marriages because people are not willing to admit they have a problem, and, more important, they are not willing to put away bad behavior. Until they do, they will continue to have problems.

A key concept to successful relationships is understanding that we can change only ourselves; we cannot change others. It's like practicing for a big game. Each player knows his job—the kicker is supposed to kick, the quarterback is supposed to throw the ball, and so forth. But if each player doesn't play his role to the best of his ability, the team will not win. If the quarterback needs to make an adjustment, only he can make it. There is nothing the guard or wide receiver can do. It's the same in a relationship. We can only adjust ourselves; we can't correct other people's problems. Sometimes, we feel obligated to make someone change or make someone do something, but we cannot make anyone change any behavior. Change comes from within. If your significant other didn't do romantic things when you were dating, and when you addressed the issue of a lack of romance, he or she still didn't change, don't expect the behavior to change when you get married. Marriage doesn't make a person change. Remember, earlier, we said marriage is a symbol of the bond and dedication you pledge to a person; it's not a magic wand that makes people perfect. Any problems that existed prior to the marriage will still exist after you say *I do*, unless you attempt to change them together during the courtship.

The two people in the relationship should address any concerning issues they have prior to getting married, and they should try to mend those concerns. Again, this process more than likely will require work by both people, but you should put in that work if the relationship is worth it. Each person should proceed with a corrective action plan when conflicting, unbearable issues are identified. This plan will tell what the problem is and offer reasonable resolutions to it.

For example, if you tell your significant other that you're not comfortable with her being friends with her ex-boyfriends, she should act to correct this problem. A corrective action plan should come with a time limit. Give your mate a specific amount of time to handle the problem. For example, give her five days to get rid of her ex-boyfriends' numbers from her phone. Once the corrective action plan is put in place, both parties are expected to respect this plan. This means that once the thirty days are up, she should not go behind your back and put the numbers back in her phone. That would be a sign that she isn't taking the relationship seriously, and she isn't ready for a committed relationship because she doesn't want to change this behavior.

It is best that you go your separate ways or take a break when one defies the corrective action plan. You cannot make a person be faithful to you, but you can make it a requirement if they want to be with you. Again, you can't make an adult do anything. *Make* means "to create, form, or cause something to exist"; we don't have that much power over someone. A requirement, however, is different. *Require* comes from the root word *re*, meaning repeatedly, and *queerer*, meaning to ask—repeatedly asking someone something for a reason. A requirement in a relationship is like the requirement the body has for food and water. If your body does not get food and water, there are dire consequences. When someone is in a motor vehicle accident, he requires medical attention. If he doesn't get the proper medical attention, he may die. A requirement is a mandate for something. Relationships should be handled no differently. You should require certain things in your relationship. If that requirement is not met, there must be dire consequences. Mandate your requirements in the relationship first. Don't surprise your mate with a long list of requirements after you get married. That will be trouble. Address the requirements beforehand, and the transition to marriage will be smoother. Any actions you ignore in the relationship/courtship, you will have to ignore in the marriage. Determine your requirements before you say *I do* to avoid heartache and headache down the road.

It is hard for someone to follow rules when we don't know what they are. It may seem like common sense not to cheat on your significant other, but like the saying goes, "Common sense is not so common." If common sense were common, people wouldn't cheat all the time. So, lay out your requirements, and then mandate them in the same way our government mandates taxes. Don't make idle threats when the rules are broken. You must enforce your relationship requirements with vigor and steadfastness. If someone treats you like you are disposable, don't stick around for that behavior to continue or to try to make the person change. Show him or her you are not disposable, and you have value. If that person doesn't want to "buy" you, he or she needs to put you back on the shelf.

Knowing your value is the key to how someone will treat you. Value is directly related to self-esteem. It takes good self-esteem to have a prosperous marriage. More than likely, if you have high value in yourself, the person you are dating will place high value in you as well. Remember, we receive what we release. A person can tell if you value your self or not.

> A well-known speaker started off his seminar by holding up a twenty-dollar bill. In the room of two hundred, he asked, "Who would like this twenty-dollar bill?"
>
> Hands started going up.
>
> He said, "I am going to give this twenty dollars to one of you, but first, let me do this." He proceeded to wrinkle the twenty dollar bill.
>
> He then asked, "Who still wants it?"
>
> Still the hands went up.
>
> "Well," he replied, "what if I do this?" And he dropped it on the ground and started to grind it into the floor with his shoe.
>
> He picked it up, now all crinkled and dirty. "Now who still wants it?" People still raised their hands.
>
> "My friends, you have all learned a very valuable lesson. No matter what I did to the money, you still wanted it because it still had value. It was still worth twenty dollars.

Many times, in our lives, we are dropped, crumpled, and ground into the dirt by the decisions we make and the situations that come our way. We feel as though we are worthless. But no matter what has happened or what will happen, you will never lose your value. You are a precious gift bought with a price; built in the image of God, the creator.

Self-esteem is your opinion of yourself. If you have had a lot of bad experiences in your life, your opinion of yourself will be low. If you have a negative opinion of yourself, then you may be letting people treat you poorly because you feel you don't deserve the absolute best. Please know this is not the truth. You deserve to be treated the very best. Low self-esteem is a thinking disorder in which we view ourselves as inadequate. Once this thought enters our minds, it radiates negative and self-defeating behavior. This negative energy defuses every essence of our being and causing us to think defeating thoughts even though we are not defeated.

The Self-Esteem Book by Dr. Joe Rubino reports that 85 percent of the world's population is affected by low self-esteem. Studies indicate that young girls who become pregnant do so because of low self-esteem, which derived from the following:

- Being a poor, disengaged student
- Lacking basic skills
- Looking for someone or something to love
- Being sexually abused
- Coming from a dysfunctional family

Self- esteem is common and we all may face it at some point in our life. But, we can overcome it. No matter what happened earlier in your life, you deserve the best in all relationships. If you feel you have self-esteem issues, you should seek help to take control of this area of your life. There are several therapeutic ways to conquer the demon of low self-esteem like meditation, prayer, hypnosis and therapy.

There are so many things that determine the success of a marriage but being centered and whole as a person is vital. Self-Realization and self-evaluation aid in securing an individual. A secure individual can secure a healthy marriage. Love and marriage is a lifetime commitment that requires a sustained sense of self. Marriage isn't love but if we believe in love, we can believe in marriage.

CHAPTER 4

Expectations of Love

Now that you're familiar with yourself, it's time to get to know the person you are courting and even more importantly, what you expect from them. When you are dating, you should access the strengths and weaknesses of your potential mates to determine if they will complement the essence of who you are. There is no perfect mate. Each person has certain strengths and weaknesses, but it is wise to access these before you get too far. You need to know if the two of you will balance each other and do you possess key attributes needed from a significant other. For example, does she keep a clean house, is she courteous, or does he have a good job.

Do we ever know someone, and if so, how well do we know that person? How honest are we with people when we are dating? Be realistic with your expectations while you are dating someone. Occasionally people are not very honest when we initially meet someone. For some reason we feel the need to make ourselves appear perfect and accomplished. We don't want people in our business, which is fair, but we feel compelled to be the ideal man or woman. Society and our ego puts pressure on us to be the best. We want to have the highest credit score, the highest-paying job, the best apartment, and the best clothes. With that said, we should not believe everything a person says when we initially meet. The real way to know people is by observing them. Pay attention to what they do instead of what they say. Simple things matter and are big indicators of someone's true intentions.

One of my friends always tells me, "You don't believe anything people say." She is right. I don't believe what people say to me; I believe what they show me. I believe what they say to other people when they think I'm not listening. I believe how they act around their friends. Truth is found in someone's actions.

A male friend once called me as I was getting off work and asked if I wanted to go out for a drink and something to eat. I thought, *that's good; I can eat and have a wonderful conversation with a friend who's cute.* When we got to the restaurant, I ordered something to eat, and he ordered a drink. I was hungry because I had just gotten off work, and it was suppertime. When we finished eating and drinking, the waiter asked how we wanted the check, and my friend said, "Separate." I was furious! I couldn't believe this clown had invited me out at dinnertime and didn't want to pay for my food. He acted as if my company was complimentary. My company is not a courtesy and if you ask me to go somewhere with you at DINNER time, you should at least pay for my meal. What an idiot. I didn't say anything to him; I just paid for my food and went home. But I was thinking, *what a jerk- how can you ask someone to go out with you and tell the waiter, OUT LOUD, you are not paying!* Really??

One thing I absolutely adore in a man is chivalry. That was my expectation while dating. "After that, I just couldn't take that guy seriously, Although I liked him, I didn't see any chivalry in him. Paying attention and observing actions goes a long way. In this case I got the feeling he was into himself, that he was his number-one priority. He had recently graduated from law school and was studying for the bar exam, so he just had his head too high in the air. A quick way for any guy to turn me off is for him not to pay for something or not pursue me. Those are big no-no's in my book. To be with me, he must pay and pursue. Pay and pursue were the magic rules.

Now I understand that he may not have had a lot of money since he was fresh out of college, but then he shouldn't have acted like I was just the "fun girl," only calling me when he wanted to have fun. No sir, that didn't work. My rule and expectation when I was dating – I am nm not the fun-girl. I knew I was the girl you should take seriously, better yet, you needed to wow me. My time was not complimentary, and every moment I choose to share with the person I was dating should be appreciated and valued.

Every single person needs to set a standard for themselves. There must be certain things you are not willing tolerate. If nothing is expected, you will get nothing in return.

As I've mentioned, when I met my husband, I had no children and he had seven. But he was honest about that; he never lied to me. I respected and admired that. People tend to be reluctant about sharing too much of themselves when they are dating because they don't want to make themselves too vulnerable. That's understandable. There is no reason why you should tell your entire life story to someone you have only been on three dates with. But when a relationship starts to turn into something more serious, you should be more transparent.

Dating is the detection phase of a relationship, and it's time to start taking serious calculations of the person you are with. Once you get older and start looking for someone to really share your life with, your list of expectations is a necessity.

In a marriage there needs to be assessment on how hard we are being on our mate. Marriage is a commitment, remember. It is symbolic of promise to love, share and protect this person while starting a family with them. In this commitment people will make mistakes and lose their way. How will you be able to handle this?

Children can be a huge part of a relationship breakdown whether they conceived during the relation or before. Statistics indicate that 8 percent of households with minor children are led by young single fathers (Belkin, 2013) From 1960 to 2011 there were 2,669 single father households in the United States (pewsocialtrends.org). In 2006 the Centers for Disease Control and Prevention did a study on men ages fifteen through forty-four and found that nearly half (47 percent) reported fathering at least one biological child in their twenties. The chance of finding a man without children is low. The opposite statistics are true for women. The US Census Bureau's population survey in 2014 indicated that 47.6 percent of women between ages fifteen and forty-four have never had children. So a man will be more likely to find a woman with no children than a woman finding a man with no children.

It's really not how many children someone has (to a certain extent) but how well he handles the situation. People seem to have kids with no strings attached. Society doesn't put a lot of pressure on people anymore to maintain a family unit, and thus, people have children freely.

How many children he had was irrelevant to me. Does anyone really accept anything, or do they learn how to deal with it? The word *acceptance* is used a lot in today's culture because it is so typical to meet people who have children—everyone wants to know if you will "accept" the children. But the reality is, a lot comes along with that. For example, there are mothers, aunts, cousins, and situations that bring pause to this theory of accepting. We accept Jesus Christ as Lord and Savior. We accept that the sun is hot. But accepting someone's children is far more complex.

In my situation, I wanted to understand the bigger picture, which was why my husband had so many children or why he even had children to begin with. It's not about accepting someone's baggage; the key is in understanding why or how they got to that point in life. You can't accept something you don't understand. Understanding why we do what we do is important. Accepting something involves giving consent to something that is true and real. Can you give consent to someone's children? The Latin form of the word *accept* means to surrender. Can we surrender to someone's children? The truth is we don't *accept*, in true form, someone's children; we learn to absorb the idea and adjust to what unfolds. We learn to love, appreciate, counsel, consider, and embrace someone's children as extension of our existence. We really can't accept; we learn how to invite others into our lives.

A man or woman may have one child and have extreme chaos, or they may have five children with no chaos. This is the true reflection of the type of person the parent is. In the ten years I've known my husband, I have never had a moment of chaos with any of his children's mothers. I have never exchanged one bad word with any of these women. He handles that situation with complete finesse. That is admirable.

When someone has children, it can be a good indicator of what type of person he or she is in general—giving, loving, forgiving, selfish, and the like. The way people treat their children can be a telltale sign of how they may treat you. Don't minimize the role someone plays in his or her child's life. My husband was an awesome father to his children, and I admired that. Another thing I admired is how close all of his children are, even though they were raised in different households. His children not only knew each other but had a close relationship with each other. That spoke volumes. If your significant other constantly argues with the child's other parent about small things, this may be a sign that he or she is immature or selfishness. If a grown person doesn't want to buy diapers, for example, how in the world can he or she pay the electric bill?

Because my husband has so many children, there are times when I face insecurity or feel left out. It reminds me of the Bible story of Abraham and his wife, Sarah. Sarah and Abraham had been married for a very long time, but Sarah could not conceive children. Out of desperation and compassion for her husband, Sarah asked her maidservant Hagar to sleep with her husband, Abraham, and conceive a child. She wanted Abraham to have a descendent and, more important, wanted to see him happy. Hagar did as she was asked; she slept with Abraham and had a son for him named Ishmael. After many years Sarah eventually had a child with Abraham, whom she named Isaac. After some time Sarah became annoyed with Hagar and her son, Ishmael, and she wanted them to leave the land so that her son, Isaac, could have all of Abraham's attention. Abraham obliged Sarah and had Hagar and her son relocate.

I can completely identify with how Sarah was feeling. There are times when you just want your own family with no outside interference. In an ideal world, no one would have any stepchildren, but of course people do. So you have to deal with the situation in the best way you can. I must continue to work on being patient and understanding so that my husband won't feel as if I am making him to choose between me and his children, I realize they need him as much as I do and but it can be a very complex and difficult situation at times. I have had to pray for wisdom and understanding so that I won't plague my marriage with negative energy.

When you are getting to know someone, you need to focus on getting to know them for you. Don't let what other people say influence you. When I was dating my husband, one of my friends was trying to hook me up with another guy. She thought he was a really "good catch" because he was a college graduate, had a good job, was attractive, and had no kids. She thought Lee had too many children and I would run into problems later on. I wasn't interested in the guy with whom my friend was trying to hook me up; there was something about him I just didn't like. I went on a lunch date with him, however, just to say I tried. And I thought maybe the date would give me a different perspective. It didn't. I'd been completely right about this guy. He was conceited. I dislike guys like that. What a turn-off; it's almost a feminine trait when men feel braggadocios about their accomplishments. I didn't care about him being an engineer or that he was smart and good-looking. He was an egotistical jerk—plain and simple. His conversation didn't keep me engaged. I can't even remember what we talked about on that boring date, but I can still remember the very first words my now-husband said to me when I first met him. Isn't that funny? Some people are supposed to be in your life, and some people are not. My friend thought that other guy was a good catch, but he wasn't a good catch for me. Sometimes people look good on paper, but they actually don't care about anyone but themselves. Don't compromise your desires for what looks good on paper or for what other people think is good for you.

I knew Lee was the guy for me after knowing him for about two years. He cared deeply for me, and he wanted to make me happy. That feeling just made me weak in the knees. Most people thought he would be trouble, but my very close friends saw the love and admiration he had for me. Even my friend who tried to hook me up with someone else, later confessed that she saw how much Lee loved me. Love happens.

Another thing that drives a wedge in relationships are untruths. It is so devastating when someone lies to you. It leaves you with a feeling of confusion and hurt. You may not know whether to be upset, angry, or just not care. A lot of the time, it depends on what people lie about—that is the determining factor. Did they lie about where they live? Did they lie about how many children they have? Did they lie about being in a relationship? Another determining factor is how many times they have been dishonest with you. Are they deceptive about everything?

Little white lies told occasionally may not be hurtful, but when occasional white lies become serial lies, you may have a problem.

We must also be aware that people can lie in different ways; for example, avoiding an issue, omitting information, giving the silent treatment as an answer, or getting angry to avoid the discussion all together. Dishonesty is a complex issue to deal with. We must evaluate people on a dishonesty scale while taking several factors into consideration. Also, consider your expectations for deception. Do you expect to be lied to?

First, we must realize that we all have told lies at some point in our lives. Most people lie to protect themselves or to protect the person to whom they are lying. People always lie with an agenda, and it is important to know their agenda. Is their intention to cover up a deceitful act so they can continue to do it, or are they lying about a previous felony charge because they are embarrassed? Knowing the motive for the lie is important in ascertaining what kind of person you are dealing with.

Second, there has to come a point of purging the lies for the sake of the marriage or relationship. Marriage is a promise based on the integrity of the two-people involved. If you cannot trust your spouse, the marriage is doomed. For example, say you have discovered that your spouse has been lying about going to work. When you confront your spouse with the evidence, it is important for him or her to give you the entire truth. Maybe your spouse has lost his or her job and is embarrassed about it. Embarrassing as it may be, however, your spouse needs to be forthcoming about the situation. Open and honest communication is the key ingredient for trust. When you purge the dishonest things that have happened during the relationship, it is important to make sure everything is divulged. It is also important that you do not return to the pattern of lying. Keep a clean slate with your significant other so that the level of trust can be maintained.

Third, you must consider the time frame of the deception. Did the lie occur prior to the marriage or relationship or after? The time frame of the lying is a sign of the intent of the person. If most of the lies occurred prior to the marriage, then maybe he or she made poor decisions while you were dating but no longer have the desire to be deceptive. Once you take these factors into consideration, you can determine if this person is worth your time.

In conclusion, knowing your expectations takes away a lot of strain in a relationship. Having your expectations in place lays a solid foundation for how your relationship should progress. People's view on life can rub off on you, so be careful with whom you surround yourself. If you are with people who always see the negative and never the positive, it will rub off on you. People with negative outlooks on life lack inspiration and don't feel deserving of something better. It is very hard to show people that they deserve better because their minds have been conditioned otherwise.

Planning an entire life with someone takes compromise and a meeting of the minds. No two people think alike on every issue, but if you plan *forever* with someone, you should think alike on more things than not. Every disagreement shouldn't become a full-blown argument. If you are a little different in some areas, it will add spice to your relationship. Spice is the key to life. As I said earlier, my husband is completely opposite of me, from the opposite side of the tracks, but he complements me. We share the same dreams for our family and children, and that's what matters most. The important thing is to recognize what you are and are not willing to sacrifice for your forever.

CHAPTER 5

Remaining in Love

Maybe you've been with someone for a while, so you are considering the next big step. Do you want to get married because it's the next phase in the relationship? Is it that you can't live without the person? That you have children together? That you're getting older and are ready to settle down? You must consider how you will stay in love. Remember you can love and care for someone but grow out of the need to be around that person. We talked about the phases of love and how hormones affect that need to be with that person. We also talked abut how people change and evolve. These changes affect our hormone levels and people lose their connection. I don't believe you fall out of love, but you can lose your connection.

Losing the romantic connection, you share with someone can be devastating, which is one thing that makes the longevity of a marriage challenging but you can do it. There are two key elements you need; Commitment and motivation.

Being committed to something is not easy because commitment leaves you vulnerable. No one likes to feel vulnerable, but vulnerability is necessary in marriage. You also need to be motivated to see your marriage through. These are key attributes that you must seriously consider before you are ready to spend the rest of your life with someone. This task may be simple for some people and extremely difficult for others.

When I got married I was twenty-seven years old and seven months pregnant. I told Lee I wanted to get married and have a family. We were already planning to get married the following year in July, but when I found out I was pregnant I wanted to move it up. The next morning he called and asked my dad for his blessing, and we got married five months later. I feel Lee had a desire to get married because deep down, he too wanted to have a child within the institution of marriage. He never told me this, but he never rejected the idea. Sometimes he jokingly says to me, "You made me marry you." I look at him and say, "I sure did." It was the next step, so there was no point in waiting.

I dislike hearing people throw out every excuse in the book not to get married. Marriage is two people coming together and making a family. It is not going to be perfect, but it is real. Marriage is not a trip to the moon or a survival of the fittest that requires a million dollars in the bank. If any couples are willing to share their lives, finances, and space, then you can do it too. There is no perfect reason why you should get married, but if you love someone and want him or her in your life, you should do the right thing.

Proverbs 18:22 says a man who "findeth a wife findeth a good thing." It's good that you have found someone willing to share his or her life with you. It is an honor for someone to say, "I like you enough to share myself and what I have with you." We should view marriage this way—as an honor. If the Bible says it's good, then it's good. Let's discuss the most important things a marriage needs to make it successful.

People may not get married if they have a fear of commitment. *Commitment* is a strong word, and everybody is not strong enough to do it. Commitment means to bind together with a pledge, a promise. When you make a commitment, you are invested in someone else. That indicates you feel whatever you are investing in holds a particular value, and you trust you will get something in return.

People invest a certain amount of money in the stock market, hoping their money will double or triple. They trust their investment will yield a reward. It's no different in a marriage. When you commit, you are investing in the idea that this person loves you as much as you love him or her, and you are now a team that will build a rewarding future together.

One of the key reasons marriages fail is lack of commitment. Earlier I mentioned the requirements in a relationship and how specific you have to be. Commitment works the same way. Don't let your partner off the hook with a vague commitment like *honor.* Honor is a given; we understand that already. True commitment should be a challenge. For example, are you willing to commit to join finances, paying the bills, and so forth? Commitment is being dedicated in every aspect of the relationship, and it requires relentless effort. Don't assume that your understanding of the commitment is the same as your mate's. Each person's perception of commitment and other concepts is different. You need to know if you are on the same page with your mate; the best way to find out is to ask. Is this individual willing to forsake all others and be committed to you and your family? "Forsake all others" is a big phrase in the marriage vows, and it means a lot. Are you willing to forsake your mom, sister, brother, and children for the betterment of your spouse? Your spouse must come first, after God, and your spouse needs to feel you are treating him or her this way.

Commitment gives you the tenacity to continue in a marriage when things seem to be falling apart. Dr. Michael P. Johnson, former sociology professor at Penn State University, analyzed three levels of commitment that affect the decision to continue in a relationship. The three types of commitment are personal, moral, and structural.

Personal commitment is centered on the idea of "I want to." When you possess personal commitment, you will find yourself saying things like "I want to continue in my marriage." Or "I enjoy being married." Personal commitment only involves you; it comes from within. This is something you desire and cherish, and you want to protect it.

Moral commitment is based on an individual's morals and beliefs. Moral commitment causes you to believe in the vows and promise you made to God, which makes you want to do the right thing. Morals are the fiber of our beings. They give us direction and guide us on our paths. When a moral commitment is made, we agree that this decision is paramount to our principles.

Structural commitment is when you believe divorce would be detrimental to your family structure. External constraints, like finances and children, keep you in your marriage. You believe in the family structure you have built, and you believe you have to keep it together. (Johnson, 2008)

All three of these commitments play a part in keeping a marriage together. The active presence of all three components makes marital resolve stronger than if only one type of commitment was present. Ecclesiastes 4:12 says, "A threefold cord is not quickly broken."

Each one of these levels of commitment contains even more layers of why a person becomes commitment or invested in a relationship. All these layers of commitments are choices and the investment you feel you have made in the relationship. During marriage, it's helpful to remember the investments you have made, and it helps you stay focused. With any commitments or investments, there is a goal. One of the goals of your marriage should be to stay married. It sounds silly, but you must make this a priority. Once this goal is clear, you must come up with a plan to maintain this goal. The three commitment components—moral, structural, and personal—should keep you on track.

An article by on Focus on the Family indicates we should strengthen and nourish our marital commitments. This can be done, for example, through prayer, actions, setting goals, and going public.

> **Prayer**—Seek God's will for your life. Ask God to show you how to be a spouse
>
> **Actions**—Let your behavior reflect your level of commitment to your marriage. Make yourself available to your spouse. Build a hedge of protection against external temptations and distractions.
>
> **Setting goals**—How would you like to see your marriage grow? You and your spouse should discuss your goals openly to make sure you are on the same page.
>
> **Go public**—Public ally announce your level of commitment to your marriage by renewing your vows (Family, 2016)

This article goes on to explain that people in a relationship must understand the depths of a marriage. It is a lifelong commitment that is a sacred and solemn mystery in the sight of God. In other words it should not be taken lightly. Two people have to work really hard and make he necessary changes and adjustments along the journey.

Have you ever met someone who was recently married, but you saw no change in that person? Everything the person did before marriage he or she still was doing. This is a person who has failed to commit to the marriage and the unity. A man may still be sneaking behind his wife's back, going out to the club, or a woman may decide to have a savings account on the side that her husband doesn't know about. If this is the case, these people are planning for the marriage to fail instead of planning for the marriage to be successful. People don't like to fully commit to some things because they are not sure they will get a full return on their investments. No matter what, commit 100 percent to your marriage, or don't get married. Then if the marriage does fail, you will carry no guilt because you will know you did your best. God requires his children to do their best, and when you do your part, God will bless you.

Some women feel having a secret bank account is a security blanket, but they are actually being dishonest. They are not committed. There may be pause in their marriages that has given them the feeling they need to do this, but if there is, that is a sign of trouble.

Be honest with yourself: is this the type marriage you want? A marriage based on unknowns and unpredictable situations will constitute an unstable environment for children. No one in a marriage should feel the need to hide anything from their spouse. When you get married, it is not just about you anymore; it's about the family and what is best for the family. Husband and wife are the heads of the family. Do you want your children raised in an environment where Mommy and Daddy keep secrets from each other?

People who lack true commitment will run as soon as things get tough. Deep down, they were planning to run the entire time. Do you have your eyes on the exit sign in your marriage instead of on God? You may be so busy planning to not get hurt in a relationship or not come out on the bottom that you lose faith in God. This comes from an insecurity that has not been addressed in your life or relationship, or maybe, deep down, you know you shouldn't have married this person (or you don't know why he or she married you). Your insecurities cause you not to trust your finances to your spouse or cause you not to delete your ex's phone number from your phone. Take your eyes off the exit sign, and stop planning for your marriage to fail. You are not a psychic, and this man or woman may not cheat on you. If he does, it's not the end of the world. You must plan for success in every area of your marriage. Condition your mind to be free of insecurities, and work for your purpose. Stop believing you should get your way. Every day isn't a sunshiny day, but if you have a spouse you can believe in and trust, you can get over any obstacle. It may fail, but it also may *not* fail, and others may look to you when your marriage works.

Commitment doesn't mean losing your identity. Stay true to yourself and who you are, but give the relationship a true effort. If you feel like you are losing yourself, you are doing something wrong. Revisit your self-realization, and remember your requirements and boundaries. Being committed doesn't mean your spouse can cheat on you without consequences. The commitment means you will be honest in your investment in the marriage, and you will do your very best to make it work. Being committed doesn't mean you're a doormat. Again, you cannot control the other person's action, but you can control yours. Commitment is a huge part of your marriage; it gives you purpose in your marriage. When you have purpose in your marriage, you will have peace.

Motivation is another key attribute you must have for a successful marriage. When you are motivated about anything, you usually are inspired to complete the task, no matter what it takes. This is the type of attitude you have to have toward your marriage. Being motivated means you believe in something, and you are passionate about it.

The easiest way to understand this concept is to think back to a time when you were motivated to do something. Were you motivated to make the football team in high school? Were you motivated to get a certain job? Whatever it was, remember the feeling you had at the time. If you were motivated to make your high school or college football team, you probably spent a lot of time practicing and getting in shape. The goal you were trying to accomplish constantly stayed in your mind, and you constantly thought of ways you could become better so that you could accomplish the task. This is the feeling you must have in your marriage. You have to constantly be motivated to see your marriage through and make sure it's a success. Think of ways to make the marriage better. Think of ways to make the marriage stronger.

Companies look for ways to motivate their employees to be more productive. Managers use different strategies to encourage employees, such as helping them to feel the work they do has meaning, that good work is rewarded, and that they are treated fairly. These strategies are no different from the strategies we should use in a marriage. We should look for ways to make our spouses feel supported, loved, and treated fairly. We should reward good behavior. Let your spouse know you appreciate him or her and that the work he or she does is important.. When your mate feels these actions, he or she will, in turn, become inspired and motivated to perform at his or her best in the marriage.

Having the desire to accomplish something clearly isn't enough. Activation, persistence, and intensity are other components required to keep going in spite of the difficulties. Activation is when you set the behavior or feeling in motion. If you know you want your marriage to be a success you should start from day of the marriage to set a positive energy in motion. Don' start your marriage with deceptive or misleading behavior and then wonder, later down the road, why your mate has insecurities. You put those insecurities in place by being deceptive. Every action receives and equal reaction. If you put a negative behavior in place you will get negative behavior in return.

Persistence is the continuing effort you apply to achieving your goal, even though obstacles will exist. Along with persistence you will need patience. If you are trying to be the most understanding wife you know how to be, and your husband is still pushing your buttons, you will have to have patience so you won't break his neck. If you have tried talking to your significant other about a potential issue and they are not hearing you, you may have to involve a neutral party. Sometime a neutral person can be the remedy to a difficult issueg

Intensity involves putting the rubber to the road and applying concentration to get the goal accomplished. A lot of times we run out of steam when we are trying to accomplish a goal, and when we get tired, we give up. But think of a runner in a race; he has to kick it into high gear at the end to cross the finish line. Intensity requires you to use your mind and focus on your goal. These three components are necessary elements for staying motivated and focused in your marriage. So many pitfalls will occur in your marriage, but motivation will inspire you to push on.

Motivation includes a constant reminder of what your purpose is. If your purpose is a long, healthy marriage (which it should be), remind yourself of this when you feel discouraged. Find a symbolic trigger to keep you motivated. For example, look at your wedding pictures, remember your first date, remember the birth of your child, and look at a Valentine's card your spouse gave you when he or she didn't have money to buy you a gift. These triggers will sometimes put an argument or disagreement in perspective and keep you focused on the success of your marriage. Unexpected actions speak volumes, putting a smile on your mate's face and keeping the marriage fresh. If your mate likes coffee, get up and fix a cup of coffee. If you do something for your wife or husband, do not expect something in return. This is a motivation killer, and it makes people put up their guards. This will lead your spouse to wonder what you want every time you do something nice. Also, don't start the routine of doing something nice only when you make a mistake. This again sends the wrong message. If you cheated on your spouse, don't automatically think a new purse or shoes will make the action go away. When you hurt someone, it takes a deeper level of actions to mend the hurt. Nice things should be done because you love someone and want to express that love. When you turn kind gestures into a mask of empty feelings, it changes the makeup of the marriage. Send clear messages in your marriage. Be on purpose in your marriage. Everything in life works better when we operate from purpose. Even surprising someone is on purpose. Purpose-driven people have more success. Move toward the goal in your marriage with purpose.

Compassion is a strong emotion that is necessary in a marriage. Having empathy for a person allows you to put yourself in the other person's shoes. Compassion means you have sympathy and concern for the suffering of others. When you possess compassion in your marriage, it means you can suffer with your spouse. Some scientific research suggests that being compassionate can improve health and well-being. Some findings say compassion makes us feel good by activating pleasure circuits in the brain and can lead to lasting increase in happiness. Another benefit of being compassionate is that it can reduce risk of heart disease by boosting the positive effects of the *vagus nerve*. The vagus nerve helps to slow down your heart rate. It is located at the top of spinal cord and travels throughout your body. It helps control the process of breathing and helps you calm down. It is also connected to oxytocin receptors in the body and is referred to as the "love nerve" in the body. Research shows that some people have a stronger vagal profile than others (Emmamseppala, 2013). This means they are more susceptible to the feeling of compassion. People who lack this profile can strengthen this response by doing meditation or exercising, which will result in more positive feelings on a daily basis. In an article on Greatergood.org, Dacher Keltner explains that showing compassion in your daily life means seeing people as individuals, not abstractions or distant objects. We should attempt to identify more with people's feelings. When we are able to identify with other people's feelings, we can understand that person on a deeper level. This serves extremely beneficial in marriage.

In a marriage, you have to practice seeing things from your partner's perspective during difficult or stressful situations. At such a time, look for ways to attend to your partner's feelings. Demonstrate the ability to care about your spouse's afflictions. It is sometimes easy to dismiss your spouse's feelings because attempting to understand them may seem too difficult. But if we practice this ritual of identifying with our partners' feelings, it will become easier to access why they feel the way they do.

I am guilty of dismissing my husband's feelings because I just forget that men have feelings too. In a discussion, I want him to listen to me, but I don't often listen to him. I struggle with this area more than anything. I tend to say what I think he *needs* to hear. I disguise my comments with the statement, "I'm just keeping real." But in doing so, I am hurting his feelings. Hurting someone's feelings is never fair. We can get our points across without hurting our spouses' feelings and making them feel less than they are.

Often in relationships, if we don't get our way, we want to forsake the commitment. Some relationships fail because two people are not willing to compromise or possibly admit they are wrong. We assume because our partners don't want to do what we want them to do, then there's no resolution. This is not true. We should train ourselves to look higher. Sometimes this means being silent. Lord knows, this is an extremely difficult task for me. It is hard to be quiet when someone is pushing all your buttons. But even in trying times, we have to learn the discipline and the principle of being quiet. Quietness allows us to see things from a deeper level, and it will prevent us from making rash decisions and saying things that we may regret. Sometimes we just have to be quiet. Lee is really good at this. He can get quiet and not say anything. It's quite amazing, actually.

Once you feel that you can truly give compassion and are motivated and commited, you may be ready to win in your relationship. Marriage is a team effort. No one can win by himself or herself. It takes two people working together.

CHAPTER 6

Be Patient with Love

In relationships, things can get tough and you will wonder, “is this relationship right for me?” Sometimes, people just don’t act how we think they should act. It causes extreme frustration when it seems you can’t get through to someone and they can’t see your way. You may even begin to question your love for this person. There is a valuable lesson is this experience called contentment. Be patient with love.

This is a valuable lesson I had to learn. No one told me my husband wasn’t going to be able to ready my mind an no one told me he views the world totally different than I do. At the beginning of our marriage, I thought he was crazy for not thinking like me. But, I have learned his difference from me makes us perfect. I had to be more patient and understanding when he had a difference of opinion from me. I wanted instant feedback and action in situations, but he wasn’t like that. He processed things differently so to ease my irritation I learned to be content and wait on my husband. I guess I didn’t know it all.

Contentment can sound like such an ugly word. It may have the connotation that you are settling for less or that you are not meeting expectations, even though you may not know what the expectation is. If someone, tells you to be content – you may think, “Be content?” Are you kidding me?” However, contentment is a virtue we must all learn to embrace if we expect to be in harmony with ourselves and others. Philippians 4:11 teaches, “For I have to be content whatever the circumstance.” Being content means standing still and knowing that whatever the situation, it will pass. I will not grumble or agonize over my problems but instead will embrace them for the learning opportunity that they are.

When you are content, you are in a state of mind that helps you endure a difficult situation. It's not a giving-up state; it's a waiting state of existence.

When you chose to complain or antagonize over what may seem to be a failure, you allow your attitude to shift to negative, thus drawing negative energy in and pushing positive energy out. Think of bad circumstances as an opportunity to exercise your "faith muscles." Bad situations are life's homework. Homework from school sometimes can take a long time to complete, but it prepares you for the test. That's what bad situations are in our lives; they are homework that prepares us for a bigger test.

God continually tries to move us to a superior level of being, but in order to know we are ready, life throws us a curve ball so God can see if we are equipped for the next level. If we change our attitudes about bad days, they won't be so bad. When your checking account is low, and you anxiously are awaiting your payday, instead of saying, "I'm tired of being broke and living check to check," say "At least I have a job and a payday to look forward to." Operate from gratitude, and your outlook will change. The universe will open up to the positive energy you release and bestow blessings on you.

In a relationship, things may get shaky due to infidelity, finances, careers, and so on, but if you invest in the success of your relationship, you will learn to keep a positive attitude. A setback is not the end of the world. You can still accomplish what you set out to accomplish; it just might take longer. Are you willing to fight for it?

Just when you think, *I really need a new car*, you look out the window and see your neighbor has a brand new Cadillac Escalade. Or just when you think, *I sure could use a vacation*, you look on Facebook and see three of your friends vacationing in the Bahamas. When you feel a slight insecurity in your life, the devil will play on this insecurity and make you feel ten times worse. This is designed to take you away from your positive force of energy and push you into the negative. When you are in a negative force of energy, you operate from a source of desperation and anger. From this source comes poor decision making. You feel self-pity and have the desire to stroke your ego. Stroking the ego is always dangerous because the ego wants the flesh to feel better, not the soul. The soul doesn't care about the neighbors having a new Escalade, but the ego does. The soul doesn't care about the Bahamas, but the ego does. So, with the ego rearing its ugly head, we feel that everything we have worked for is worthless. The two academic degrees we have on the wall, the healthy children we have, the stable job—all of it suddenly means nothing. This is because we stepped away from our area of contentment and positive thinking. Remember there is always something in our lives to be thankful for.

Don't be confused and think that being content means you are not planning to move forward. It means quite the opposite. Contentment means "I have made it this far, and I will be happy on my path, as I plan to go further." Content means "I am satisfied with how God has blessed me thus far." Contentment is a healthy tool that is used to keep our focus sharp and self-assuming. We understand we don't operate on our will but the will of God, and as long as we work on completing the plan he has for our lives, he will carry us to the next phase of our lives when he knows we are ready.

In a relationship, there are cycles that may cause your mate to act differently or choose a different path, but this doesn't mean the relationship has to end because the path has changed. During the course of life we should all change and evolve. Change is what life is about. Some change may be good; some change may be bad, but each cycle of change is designed to prepare us for the next phase of our journeys. Remember, we already talked about how people change and evolve every seven years. So expect change and be content with it.

Sometimes you may go down a path of hardship. Unfortunately, it happens to us all, but we don't give up. We fight through the hardship. When we see a change in our mates, that may be a good time to talk. We should not immediately assume change is something negative; sometimes change is a good thing. It just might be a sign of a spiritual awakening. Be optimistic and open when you see new things going on in the marriage; it just might mean your marriage is alive and evolving into the marriage it is destined to be.

Do an evaluation of where your relationship is now and where you two see it in the future. The goals you had in place five years ago may need to change. Maybe your husband no longer wants to work for someone. He may feel it's time to open his own business, and he may need your support in this endeavor. Change is a hard thing to talk about, but it is something that is inevitable. Make it a habit to sit down and discuss the direction of your relationship from time to time. You should discuss the plans and desires you have for your children, finances, and so forth. It is healthy to know how your mate feels about these things so you two can work together to achieve these goals. If one person in the relationship feels isolated or alone, he or she will look for solstice somewhere else. Be open with your mate about your expectations, and then find common ground. It is not possible that you two will agree on every goal, but you can agree to compromise on some things. You may feel that it's not the time for your mate to start a business, for example, but if it is something about which your mate is passionate and is willing to put in the work to do, who are you to stop it?

Job in the Bible lost everything; he had nothing left to give when the devil was finished with him, but as God promised, if we lose anything for His sake, He will return it to us double. If you lose something due to starting a business, God will restore your loss. In our relationships, we have to keep the faith and know that God loves marriage; it is one of His favorite things. If you are married or are about to get married, God is pleased with that. God will bless anything that pleases him.

We can't focus on what people post on Facebook or Instagram; these are illusions. People only post good things about themselves on social media. People don't post when they overdraw their bank accounts or when they get fired. Just know that the world in which we live is an illusion, and people only let you see what they want you to see. Don't think others' lives are grand because all of their filtered photos on Instagram look so glamorous; it simply is not true. You may endure a hardship, but everyone else is enduring hardships too. The difference is in knowing where your help comes from.

When operating from contentment, you allow the faith muscles to strengthen and take a shape of their own. If you exercise them enough, they will be able to take over without your executing them. When any area of doubt arises in your life, you will be able to immediately go to a realm of gratitude instead of pity. According to Amit Amin of HappierHuman.com, there are thirty-one benefits to possessing gratitude, and all of the benefits lead to a happier you. Some of these benefits include better health, better attitude, and better interpersonal relationships (Amin, 2016). All you need is to be so ever grateful for what you have and it could change the world around you drastically.

There have been several research studies that have required the participants to keep a gratitude journal. In 2007 there was the Gratitude: Effects on Perspectives and Blood Pressure study, which found that when patients with hypertension were instructed to count their blessings once a week, there was a significant decrease in their systolic blood pressure (Amin, 2016). In 2005 the Positive Psychology Process study found a gratitude visit reduced symptoms of depression by 35 percent for several weeks and keeping a gratitude journal lowered symptoms by 30 percent. A gratitude visit is an exercise where a person identifies someone they are grateful for and they write a letter and send the letter to the person in person. The idea behind the gratitude visit is show or express thankfulness to someone that you may nor have properly thanked in the past (What is a Gratitude Visit, 2016)

There is even reason to believe gratitude can increase your lifespan overtime. "Research by UC Davis psychologist Robert Emmons, author of *Thanks! How the New Science of Gratitude Can Make You Happier*, shows that simply keeping a gratitude journal—regularly writing brief reflections on moments for which we're thankful—can significantly increase well-being and life satisfaction." Gratitude has so many positive benefits on life. Just this simple frame of mind can literally transform key areas in your life.

A 2014 article on Forbes.com offered key benefits to practicing an attitude of gratitude. The article stated, "Grateful people are more likely to behave in a prosocial manner, even when others behave less kind, according to a 2012 study by the University of Kentucky. Study participants who ranked higher on gratitude scales were less likely to retaliate against others, even when given negative feedback. They experienced more sensitivity and empathy toward other people and a decreased desire to seek revenge." This type attitude is priceless in a marriage or relationship. When you find yourself getting upset or frustrated you may have to practice some of these techniques; which help you remember why you love this person and even more importantly, why you married them.

During disagreements, we may hit below the belt because we are hurting and want to say something to express how much we are hurting. But that's not fair in any argument. We should attempt to identify where the other person is coming from instead of lashing out. By implementing the gratitude effect, we'll be less likely to lash out in anger and more likely to have compassion for the other's person feelings. Arguments escalate because we feel we are not being heard or understood. Opening our hearts to gratitude and contentment will allow us to let in the softer side of ourselves and to feel less inclined to punch back when we feel attacked.

In relationships we must remember there are no perfect people.

Even you are your own form of chaos. You have just been that way so long that you think it's normal. But who's to say what's normal? You meet someone, and you feel the inclination to turn that person into a different form of you; you expect him or her to consume your beliefs, thoughts, actions, likes, and dislikes. But that is not the goal in life. The goal is to be the best you that you can be, and then your positive energy will attract others with traits that complement yours. After traveling through your self-evaluations, you should be more in touch with yourself. The journey is not about seeking who you need to change or influence but attracting people that supplement your soul's chemistry. That is the essence of a committed relationship.

We are entangled humans moving through life, embodying each other's energy. We are not perfect, and the people we meet will not be perfect. Perfection is an illusion often sought after but unobtainable. The person you meet may have children, a criminal record, an over-zealous mother, or more. Everyone who has traveled this earth has done things of which he or she is not necessarily proud. But this does not mean we should be condemned for a mistake for the rest of our lives. Sometimes other people's mistakes were made out loud, and your mistakes were quiet; that is often the only difference. Someone may not know that you had an abortion at sixteen or that you wrote bad checks when you were in college. People are flawed; don't be so quick to judge.

This entire book is about you taking steps to do this discovery so that your spirit can do the hard work for you. When you align with *yourself*, you are instantly in the vibration/path of meeting your "life partner," according to ForeverConscious.com. If you listen to your spirit and soul, it will guide you to your complementary partner. All you have to do is be available and open to the possibilities.

All in all, we should not be so quick to filter people out of our lives when it appears from the surface a certain person may not be the best catch. That person may have a heart of gold that is simply guarded. We let our checklists get in the way sometimes. When two souls are connected, there is no end to what that bond can inspire.

A real relationship is when two people get together and make a conscious effort to move toward a positive force. The imperfections of two people can complement each other. They can make up for the shortcomings of each partner. Give a person a chance and see where he or she is in the universe. The best practice is to let things flow. If you feel a connection, you owe it to yourself to see where the relationship goes. Take it step by step, and be honest and transparent. Take yourself off the high horse, and be human. Treat every experience as an authentic encounter that represents a force of nature in your life. You need these experiences to cultivate the love for which your soul and consciousness yearn.

As I stated earlier; marriage is simply two people committing their future together—nothing more, nothing less. In this sharing there will be shifts, and the success of your relationship depends on how you handle these shifts. Love is tricky, but it can be mastered. Remember that love is a living thing. Dr. Laura Berman's theory of quantum love suggests that we can manifest the feeling we want to feel in our relationships. In her book *Quantum Love: Use Your Body's Energy to Create the Relationship You Desire*, Dr. Berman provides readers with tools to cultivate the desired relationship reality they want to experience. In relationships, Dr. Berman suggests we do not have to operate from a place of feeling without but instead should operate from a feeling of abundance and create the desired feelings we seek in the relationship.

Through a series of meditation exercises that connect you with your core, you can create the feelings you want from within. You will not be perfect, but this theory suggests you can create the end result you want. Quantum love is manifesting the reality you want to live. Instead of focusing on what your spouse is not giving you, focus on ways you can inspire this in him or her.

A quote from her study:

> My patient Mary had identified her five core desired relationship feelings and I noticed they were all pertaining to a sense of stability and cooperation with her partner. She wanted to feel as though they were parenting as a team. This desire had informed much of the work we had been doing together and the work Mary

was doing on her own. She had made great strides in just a few short weeks. However, while she had seen great improvement in her relationship, she still felt like she was missing something in their connection. She just didn't know what it was. On my advice, she moved herself into home frequency and asked these questions of her essential self. The response she got wasn't what she expected at all: "I'm getting that I want adventure and romance."

I asked her to describe what she might want that to look like. "What would feel adventurous?"

She thought for a moment and said, "If Ted suddenly planned a surprise date."

I asked her to close her eyes, ground herself, open her heart and imagine: What would it feel like to be there? I walked her through the motions of entering into this new feeling state by putting herself into the scene and imagining it in the first person. Then, once she was in that mental space, I asked her to start using her senses to describe how she was feeling as she experienced the surprise date with her partner.

She said she could feel the excitement

"Well, he loves to try new food. Actually, just the other day we were deciding where to get dinner and I figured we'd go to our usual Italian restaurant but he wanted to go to this new Ethiopian restaurant. I didn't expect it from him at all, but we had a really good time."

I encouraged her to focus on the things that Ted did that were adventurous. "When he does them again," I said, "tell him how much you appreciate them and how much they turn you on."

Mary acknowledged she knew she needed to compliment his efforts more.

I congratulated her for being willing to see how her behavior might unintentionally impact Ted negatively.

This was huge to acknowledge she isn't perfect. We talked earlier, how hard it is to admit there are things you need to change. As you can see from the study, it can be liberating and give you a new frame of mind.

> Dr. Bauhmin goes on to say "One common problem I see with couples is that they look to 'convict' each other rather than to 'acquit' each other.
>
> Then I asked Mary the big question that sits at the crux of achieving your Quantum Love Goals: Have *you* been adventurous? What's keeping you from planning the surprise date?
>
> She balked. "Dr. Berman! I don't think that's very romantic."
>
> "What isn't?"
>
> "Asking me to do all the work and planning," she complained, "I want to be wooed and charmed off my feet, not the other way around."
>
> "Why is that?"
>
> "Because that is how I will know that he loves me and desires me."
>
> "And does he know that you love and desire him?" I ask.
>
> She shrugged. "He's a man, he doesn't care."
>
> She looked up sheepishly knowing she had overstated, as I confirmed, "I have never once had a man walk through my door that didn't care about feeling loved and desired. Your positive energy will inspire him to give you exactly what you want. He's going to want to get you alone. He's going to remember you when he walks by the flower shop. He's going to think of you when he sees a sexy negligee."

The essence is, again, that you have the power to create the reality you want in life and relationships. There is no reason to feel you are the victim because whatever you see lacking in life can be created through you. Remember, we don't want to manifest negative feelings but instead trigger positive vibrations. You have the power to put positive forces to work in your domain. So what if the person you are dating doesn't make eighty thousand dollars a year right now. It doesn't mean that can't happen. You can turn that frog into Prince Charming.

Remember there are attributes you possess that your spouse may also like to change, so every person is a work in progress. Improvement is only made when each person takes responsibility for the part he or she plays. You can't manipulate your mate, but you can empower him or her to be the vessel you need to accomplish your purpose. You and your mate are evolving spirits in the universe that long for truth and accuracy; your presence in each other's life can enrich this experience. Be open to the movement and patterns that your life together creates, and receive all evolution as your chosen path. Unpleasant movement is a learning experience that enhances your being. With patience, dedication, and commitment, you and your mate can become the love filled beings you were created to be.